GOULD EVANS
LIVE LEARN WORK PLAY

GOULD EVANS
LIVE LEARN WORK PLAY

Preface 6

Introduction 8

Truman Presidential Library & Museum 14

Stevie Eller Dance Theatre 20

Cerner Corporation Campus 26

Adelphi Commons 32

First Covenant Church 36

College of Business Administration 40

Eccles Center for Performing Arts 44

Grandview Community Center 48

The Biodesign Institute 52

Baron BMW 58

Rinker Hall School of Building Construction 62

Johnson County Library, Blue Valley 66

Pearson Hall School of Education 70

First United Methodist Church 74

Athletes' Performance Institute 78

Cedar City Public Library 82

East Campus Student Union 86

Love of Christ Lutheran Church 90

SALT Center 92

Bleujacket Restaurant 96

St. Paul's United Methodist Church 98

Arts & Technology Complex 102

Indian Creek Community Church 104

Palo Verde Library & Maryvale Community Center 106

Riverside School for the Arts 108

Bentonville High School 110

The Power of We 112

Credits 114

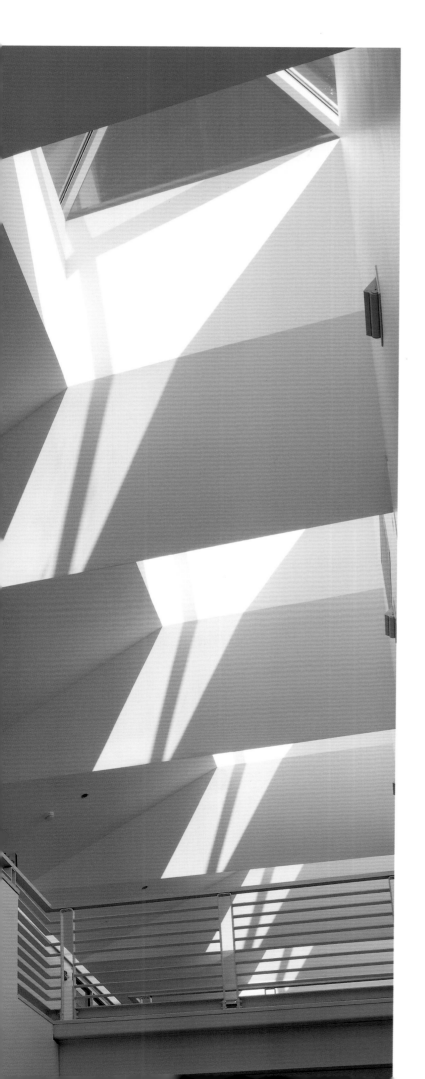

Architecture For People
by Kira Gould

Since the firm's founding in 1974, Gould Evans' designers and project teams have pursued excellence in architecture. Thinking about the people who will live, learn, work, and play in the resulting spaces and places has focused the design teams and made the work enjoyable and successful. Working closely with clients and stakeholders and pushing past conventional ideas—always looking for deeper, more powerful ways to express big ideas—has made quality, meaningful architecture possible.

Early on, the firm emphasized the collaborative nature of practice as central to the design process. Firm leaders have defined and refined the Gould Evans charrette—an intensive, highly articulated collaborative workshop. Today, many firms cite collaboration as an important part of their approach, but often they are talking about glorified meetings. We continue to develop our truly collective approach: pushing for real collaboration and open communication. Our charrettes are still the beginning of the opportunity for the design team, with the clients and stakeholders along for the ride, to live in, learn about, work on, and play with the projects themselves.

Collaboration can be messy and complex. But far from being negatives, these characteristics can create an environment that allows a divergent thought or minor conversation to ripen into a project linchpin. The element of surprise in the creative process can be tremendously rewarding to those involved. Collaborating with other architects can also be compelling, and we have been fortunate to work with peers we greatly respect. We are proud to have teamed with dozens of firms from all over the country and the world and we are proud of the resulting work, including five such projects in this volume.

Internally, we build teams with an eye toward strong communication and set them up to capitalize on the experience and strengths of each person. The creative process is different for every person and every team; this variation is what brought many of us to the field of architecture and keep us enamored with its vibrant possibilities. When allowed to flourish, that process allows inspiration, bold thought, and iteration. Exposing and documenting the creative exploration that is part of every strong project is illuminating for all involved.

Architecture, the result of this process, should always be beautiful. This may have the ring of oversimplification or self-serving platitude, but without beauty, how can the designed environment be humane, healthy, meaningful, or worth keeping? Beauty directly informs human experience. Our process engages the possibilities for beauty at each phase; even when practical matters are at hand, such as the details of programming, beauty is a part of the dialogue. How people will inhabit and use a building, what they will see when they look at it or out from it, how it will feel when they touch it, and whether they care about it enough to care for it—these questions are central.

One of the best ways to make beautiful architecture is to be honest with materials. Using materials honestly is something that our design teams feel passionate about, and this is evident in the work. Understanding the nature of steel, wood, and stone is critical to producing quality architecture that has value to the client and to anyone who visits or dwells in the building for years to come. Our teams work hard to understand the materials and detail their use explicitly.

Part of our process is about going deeper. Bold, deep thought is central to a process that yields excellence and innovation. Together our teams find the cogent design concepts with the power to keep the entire team focused and inspired throughout the project. For architecture to stand the test of time, it must have a strong underlying concept based in the elemental principles of human spirit and geometry.

The firm was founded in the 1970s, when awareness and interest in regionalism and its importance to architecture were on the rise. This approach to architecture began as a movement against placelessness and lack of meaning in architecture, and it draws heavily on phenomenology. Aspects of these ideas are infused in the firm's approach to architecture and are evident in the diversity of the work emanating from several offices around the United States.

These are not branches; they operate as independent, linked offices, designing for their communities and regions in their own way. There are commonalities: they value context and emphasize climate, topography, and tectonic form. Because we operate offices in the Midwest, Southeast, Southwest, mountain states, and the West, our design teams draw on a diverse set of contexts, experiences, and influences. We encourage our talented associates to "cross-pollinate" between offices. Encouraging regional diversity is valuable to our people, to each project, and to the body of work as a whole.

When a building or any other design responds more fully to the realities bearing upon it, the result is inherently more beautiful. The typical 20th-century building ignores its environmental surroundings and attempts to overpower them through artificial systems. A building designed with sustainability in mind uses the flux in climate, seasons, sunlight, earth temperature, and watershed management to its advantage. Rather than raging against the storm outside, the green building embraces it. In the 21st century, new technologies and new concerns abound. Our evolving world requires that we make the most forward-thinking choices.

Our design teams seek creative, integrative concepts and solutions that meet three levels of sustainability: physical sustainability (is it low-embodied energy or recyclable?), institutional sustainability (is its production helpful to society?), and spiritual sustainability (is it timeless and ennobling so people want it to last?).

We understand that designing to meet a holistic definition of sustainability is a complex, multi-layered process that involves exploration of land use, site ecology, community and regional context, water use, energy performance and transition to renewable sources, light and air, materials and construction methods, long-term value, and adaptability. Each one of these areas is complex. Seeing all sides is critical and doing so is difficult, but it never fails to contribute to the quality of the project.

Our daily opportunity is to take advantage of each and every contribution we make to the built and human environment. Each project involves hundreds of choices. Our knowledge base is utilized to develop ideas about how to powerfully bind the project to its social and physical environment. We have drawn on climate, indigenous materials, and state-of-the-art technologies to create an architecture that is definitively of its place.

Our teams are made up of curious and intellectual leaders who have a vision for their projects and a larger vision about architecture's role in making a better world and a healthier planet. Each day, they live, learn, work, and play—a spirited and fun exchange is part of what helps us express creativity as architecture—to generate quality spaces and places. The goal is architecture that serves its people and place by being a beautiful, durable, valuable asset to those who spend time there, and to the street, region, and ecosystem of which it is a part. We are grateful to the clients who have allowed us to engage their projects and whose visions have allowed us to expand our own.

If You're Cold, Add Layers
by Thomas Fisher

When asked to describe the work of his firm, Gould Evans, principal Anthony Rohr calls it, "warm modernism," an apt description that reveals a lot about their architecture as well as about the architects. "Warmth" refers not just to temperature, appropriate for a firm that works largely in the South, West, and central Midwest. Nor does it just apply to the firm's frequent use of earthy materials or its creation of light-filled interiors, all of which warm the forms and spaces they design. The word "warm" also suggests qualities such as liveliness and vigor on one hand, and intimacy and affection on the other—apparently opposite traits that often get joined in the work of Gould Evans.

The firm does this, almost unconsciously, through a strategy of layering. At one level, all buildings consist of layers or assemblies of materials that, among other things, keep warmth in or out. And, at another, more esoteric level, layering offers an effective way of dealing with differences, allowing like and unlike things to coexist in proximity to each other. But in the architecture of Gould Evans, one can see the firm consistently using the layering of materials, forms, and spaces in plan and elevation to enwrap buildings, creating greater community or connection, or to unwrap buildings, generating greater dynamism or openness.

Gould Evans has organized itself along these same lines. Founded in 1974 by Robert Gould and David Evans, the firm has transformed itself into a 200-person firm with offices in seven Midwestern, Southern, and Western cities. "From 1988 to 1998," says Robert Gould, "we had 30 to 50 percent growth each year, after which we leveled off at our current size." The firm did not merge or acquire other offices to achieve this growth, but started each office from scratch, layering the new offices onto the existing structure in order to respond to clients and conditions in particular areas. "The great thing about this," says principal Jay Silverberg, "is that there is not signature style to our work. Each office responds to its local culture and clients, continually searching for ways to raise the bar for all our design teams. Part of our collaborative process involves encouraging a collective quest for excellence." There's nothing like a little friendly competition to warm things up.

Gould Evans also warms up for projects through intensive, multi-day workshops in which the architects elicit the aspirations and goals of their clients. "We do these workshops," says Gould, "because it is always better to have clients involved, and it saves time in the long run by our understanding their needs." This process not only generates a lot of information and ideas, but it can also give the end result a more nuanced quality. "We dive into projects without knowing the answers," says principal Steve Clark, "allowing the process to provide answers in a rigorous form of discovery." This openness applies to the process itself. "We're reinventing the

workshop process," adds Clark, "because different clients have different interests in participation." Clients' organizations often have as many layers as their buildings.

While this strategy of layering doesn't give a uniform appearance to the work of Gould Evans, the firm's buildings provide an almost complete catalog of how this approach can solve a multitude of problems and create new opportunities. Look at the firm's addition to the Truman Presidential Library and Museum, for instance. The design captures new exhibition space and creates a new backdrop for the eternal flame above President Truman's grave through the simple act of placing a new layer—a curved stone wall—in front of an inside corner of the building's façade. To separate this addition, visually, from the original building, the team elevated a part of the new wall on low columns at one end to reveal part of a window behind it, and contrasted the smooth stone of the new wall against the rugged ashlar of the existing building, emphasized by a layer of raking light that filters down from a continuous skylight. It's a simple, dignified, and modest solution, appropriate to the directness and warmth of Harry Truman.

Layering can also be a way of expressing the dynamic and complex world of modern corporations, evident in Gould Evans' addition to the Cerner Corporation campus. To give the company a new icon expressive of its energy and optimism, the architects have created a spiraling entry pavilion, wrapped in layers of glass and metal that spiral up to a tower. At the same time, the designers have expressed the company's movement by peeling away layers of the landscape in a series of stepped pools and terraces, and peeling off layers of glass-walls along the façade to reveal the circulation of people inside. It all seems symbolic of the way in which companies are taking things apart to transform themselves.

Layering can express other ideas as well. In the firm's design for the BleuJacket restaurant, they use curving layers of curtains and undulating layers of booths in contrast to the exposed limestone walls and timber ceiling of the building. The Baron BMW showroom evokes layers of a different sort: the zones of movement and stasis along a highway, with projecting rooms containing individual cars along a curving customer path, like cars parked along a road. And for Stevie Eller Dance Theatre, Gould Evans echoes the movement of the dancers with a series of folded acoustical panels inside the auditorium that emerge to become a layer of metal scrims that shade the glass-walled dance studio, elevated above the glass entry lobby on several angled columns. Layering, here, provides an extraordinary degree of expression in an inexpensive and inspired way.

Gould Evans' architects also use this strategy to create a sense of community among people. The Adelphi Commons Sorority Housing consists of layers of social interaction, with a public lawn area, semi-public entry courts, semi-private chapter rooms and private courtyards that open up back to the main commons. The alternating bands of calm exterior spaces and exuberant building forms, with their popped-up roofs and pulled-out bays, also express the complexity of relationships and behaviors that characterize college communities. The Biodesign Institute, designed in association with Lord, Aeck & Sargent, achieves community in a different way, with a long, linear atrium along which people can see inside the labs, out to the circulation space, and down to the gathering space. Those internal zones of interaction get expressed on the building's exterior with layers of metal shading devices, indented walls, and projecting roofs that represent the dynamics of the work within. Layering can also beckon people into a community, as in the East Campus Student Union—a glassy building surrounded by metal scrims, covered patios, projecting banners, and overhead glass doors that reach out to the campus to invite students in—and in the SALT Center—a masonry building with balconies and breezeways that draw students into the shady courtyard where students gather.

Environmental concerns also drive many Gould Evans' buildings. In a joint venture with the Croxton Collaborative, Gould Evans designed Rinker Hall as a double-layered building, with a brick screen wall visually connecting the structure to the brick campus, and wrapping two sides of a metal-and-glass building, whose envelope expels heat quickly. Meanwhile, in the Palo Verde Library and Maryvale Community Center, designed in association with Wendell Burnette Architects, assemblies of environmentally responsible materials—cork, rubber, oriented strand board—echo the layering of the plan into various day lit spaces. Another sustainable strategy in Gould Evans' work involves multi-functional buildings. At their Love of Christ Lutheran Church, the firm constructed less building by creating a worship space that doubles as a gymnasium and performance hall, while at the Riverside School for the Arts, the firm designed spaces to have very different functions at different times of the day.

In other Gould Evans buildings, a single architectural element organizes the various activities within. At the Athletes Performance Institute, a broad curved roof reflects the movement of athletes from the entry through a layer of support spaces into the large, glass-walled training space at the back. At the Grandview Community Center, Gould Evans and Ankeny Kell Architects use the metaphor of a grove, adding layers of angled, tree-like columns and dappled-light clerestories along the main circulation routes. And in the addition to the St. Paul's United Methodist Church, the analogy of the building to a bridge, arcing over a ravine, provides a layer of circulation that reorients the entire site toward space for future growth.

While varied in appearance, all of these buildings interpret clients' diverse needs through a common strategy, flexible enough to address a wide range of conditions and yet clear enough to hold together a wide range of work. That approach may not always attract the media, which often likes more stylistically consistent approaches, or appeal to those few clients who want signature buildings by design stars. But layering gives Gould Evans' architecture a sense of liveliness and intimacy that the firm's many repeat clients must warm to, since they keep coming back for more.

Truman Presidential Library & Museum
Independence, Missouri

LEARNING HISTORY   The original Harry S. Truman Presidential Library was the first facility created under the provisions of the 1955 Presidential Libraries Act. Its goal was to preserve historical materials relating to President Truman and to make them available in a place suitable for exhibit, research, and learning. The facility sits on a 16-acre, park-like setting in a residential area of Independence, Missouri, a few blocks from Truman's long-time residence. The building is 100,000 square feet on two levels wrapped around a central courtyard.

A major renovation and addition was designed to position the institution to fulfill its broadening mission. The library and museum needed more primary exhibit space, upgraded learning environments, and an improved relationship with exterior spaces and grounds. Reinforcing the library's public image was an important goal; this included bringing the public areas of the museum to the highest standard of excellence. A curved wall allowed a circular exhibit path in a previously narrow space; this widened area leads to the feature gallery space and also created a functional indoor connection between galleries and conference center. This also improved the relationship of interior spaces to the courtyard and gravesite; a large window wall visually connects the Presidential Gallery to the courtyard.

A new White House Decision Center on the lower level serves a library goal to broaden programming for students. It was the vision of the library's former director, Larry Hackman, that the library become more proactive about its educational mission. The project shows originality in how it enabled the museum to change its approach and become a more proactive, "living" institution without changing its appearance so greatly that it would move away from its history and legacy, both reinforced by the presence of the gravesite. The improvements have a high degree of flexibility, a focus on visitor experience, space for youth education, and the full complement of scholar amenities.

The sensibility of the project is serene and sturdy, with a reliance on masonry materials and clean lines. This aesthetic allows the gravesite and eternal flame to remain the focus, while providing an elegant, powerful backdrop. By using the visitor experience as the central focus of the design approach, the resulting project crafts that experience in a special way as it relates to the story being told, the issues of that time in history, and the setting.

1. A new layer of smooth limestone masonry wall contrasts with the original textured stone. A single opening permits visual linkage of a new exhibition space and the gravesite courtyard. 2. Since the expansion and renovation, the courtyard has become more integrated into the interior experiences of the facility. 3. Natural light washes the variegated stone wall of the new exhibition space. 4. The clean simplicity of the curving wall introduces a note of elegance and solemnity to the courtyard.

3

4

5. The composition is purposefully straightforward and honest, as the man it honors was known to be.

5

Stevie Eller Dance Theatre
Tucson, Arizona

A STUDY IN MOVEMENT   For the design of the Stevie Eller
Dance Theatre, the Gould Evans design team learned about
dance, about movement, about graphically representing
dance through notation, formally called labanotation. They
immersed themselves in the idea of movement. The faculty
taught them about dance, while designers taught the dancers
about structure; together they came up with dancing columns.
The client team discussed "Serenade," the first ballet George
Balanchine wrote for the students of the School of American
Ballet. The designers studied in detail the labanotation and
score for "Serenade" and overlaid the starting positions for
each movement to create a matrix from which emerged a grid
of tilted columns. These columns support the glass-encased
dance studio on the second floor of the building.

The designers felt that the architecture should express
movement—the central focus of this learning environment.
The soft upholstered space of the auditorium is a volume that
rolls and moves to become an exterior surface that protects
the glazing of the dance studio as a scrim. The stage is a
dark backdrop upon which performers play. Inside becomes
outside as the mass of the house and stage fly tower become
the dark backdrop upon which the scrim pieces play. The
team studied how inside volumes become outside surfaces
through topology and introduced the idea of a three-
dimensional mobius strip. This was the form-generating
device for the inside and the outside of the building.

The collaboration between builder and architect during the
construction of the Stevie Eller Dance Theatre was
extraordinary. The form-generating concepts of the building
inspired the steel workers, who studied the Gould Evans
diagrams and created finely wrought wire-frame drawings.
The steel workers became part of the creative process, too;
the idea of the master craftsman re-emerged. The creative
process is the bridge that connects each member of the
team. The result is a functioning work of art.

1. The primary dance studio is a glass-walled volume wrapped in an angular steel scrim; columns below are arranged in a pattern derived from a Balanchine dance notation. 2. The airy rehearsal space is flooded with daylight filtered through the scrim that wraps the building; from inside, the metal is a transparent frame (reflected in the mirrored wall). 3. In the glass-walled ground floor lobby, mobile control screens can be set up as electronic kiosks, display panels, or shaped into a booth that is staffed for performance. 4. The performance facility seats 300 people. A series of shifted planes form the shell of the space, creating a dynamic environment without distracting the focus from the stage.

3

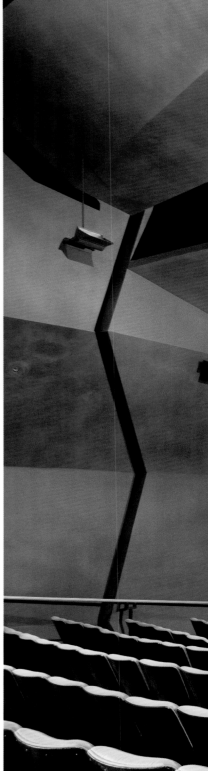

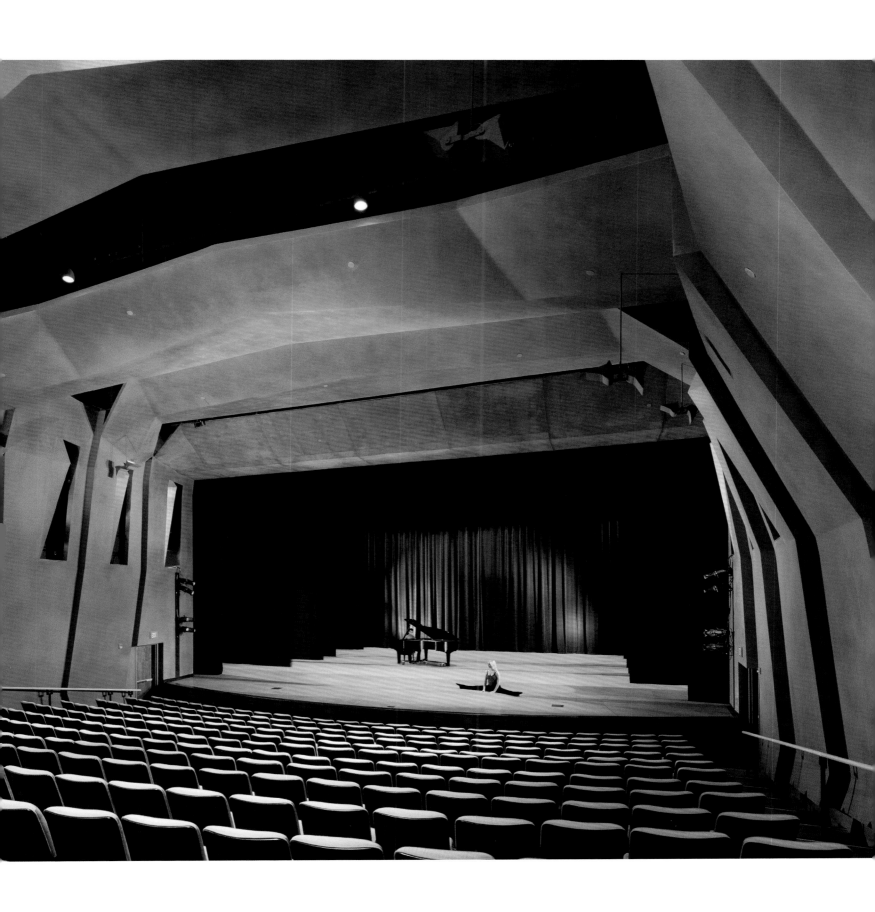

5. The metal scrim gives the building a mutating presence; at night, the volume has a dramatic transparency and the bold-hued scrim seems muted. 6. The scrim that defines the building's distinctive façade also serves as a shading device.

6

Cerner Corporation Campus
Kansas City, Missouri

THINKING FORWARD The company wanted to give its campus headquarters a world-class look, feel, and functionality. Campus master planning was followed by renovations, new facilities, and dramatic site improvements. The project centered on translating corporate attributes—vision, leadership, innovation, identity, stability, knowledge, transformation, technology, and functionality—into design elements that would be seen as company icons.

The transformation included a new headquarters building that links two existing structures and serves as the corporate "front door," a new guest/client orientation and education center (the Vision Center), an icon tower, the complete renovation and re-cladding of two office buildings, new dining and auditorium spaces, new gardens and grounds, and a complete identity and signage system for the campus.

Creating a humanistic workplace was a high priority. Talented people are in demand; keeping them happy is an important aspect of the headquarters. Workspaces benefit from natural light and are flexible and customizable; nearby, varied spaces promote ad hoc teaming. Service cores at the perimeter encourage casual interaction at the center of each floor. A raised floor system delivers air, power, and data to some work areas, providing operational flexibility and efficiency.

Intensive charrettes involved executive staff, the facilities management team, project engineers, and other consultants. The chairman spent time immersing the design team in the attributes of the company and illustrating how they drive the company. Each design decision was founded in the architects' deep understanding of the attributes. The company leaders and the design team knew that they had to create a workplace that was also a learning environment. Company growth meant that many aspects of the project were moving targets. Because of the relationship and strong communication between the company and design teams, the project was able to accommodate this fluidity.

The quality of the new and renovated spaces has improved associate morale, which has positively impacted productivity and improved retention rates. Recruiting has stepped up; the campus and amenities are selling points. The project has contributed to an increased speed to market, which relates to higher sales rates and higher overall revenues. The quality of the environment better positions the company to succeed.

1. Exterior improvements include outdoor seating, a fountain, lighting, walkways, and landscaping that bring the buildings together as a true campus. 2. Contrasting materials express the attributes of the company: stainless steel was used to depict technology, glass to depict vision, and natural warm-tone stone to depict stability. 3. The large, comfortable dining area offers on-campus meal options to busy associates. 4. Meticulously detailed metal-and-glass cladding makes a contemporary statement.

3

4

5

A

7

Experience **Vision**

"We believe Cerner has the right
strategic vision and architecture
for the future..."

Merrill Lynch & Co.
CIO Surveys
May and July 2002

Experience
CERNER

5. The 188-foot icon tower was inspired by the DNA double helix, and is wrapped by stainless steel panels with binary code perforations, symbolizing a fusion of the body and technology.
6. Thresholds to key client education spaces are large enough for two people to enter together comfortably. 7. Meeting rooms are designed to be comfortable for small or large groups.
8. Metalwork was an especially important aspect of the architectural expression, from the icon tower to signage and sunshades. 9. The 123,000-square-foot world headquarters building links two existing buildings and serves as the new front door.

Adelphi Commons
Tempe, Arizona

1

STUDENT NEIGHBORHOOD   The Adelphi Commons Sorority Housing complex at Arizona State University redefines student living and sorority life by redefining the sorority house itself. Traditionally, sororities are housed in renovated single-family residences near the campus, a condition that prevents the groups from being part of the community and limits interaction between sororities. ASU's sorority members previously lived within a multi-story residence hall on campus where each sorority occupied its own floor.

Adelphi Commons offers a hybrid solution to two conditions: establishing community and maintaining autonomy within one complex in order to create a different kind of sorority row. Individual chapter rooms within the housing complex allow each sorority to be identified. These distinct living spaces are knit together as one community within which each sorority participates as part of a collective whole.

Housing 400 students, Adelphi Commons holds 12 connected sororities organized along a pedestrian street and a large common central lawn. Each sorority has its own enclosed front yard serving as the exterior living room for each house, which allows students to engage the courtyard as an outdoor study space. Individual study areas within the bedrooms that surround the courtyard are visually connected to this outdoor space and encourage social interaction that defines daily student mode functions within the house.

The chapter house adjacent to the courtyard provides a formal venue for chapter meetings, and also serves as an informal space to lounge with friends. Glass doors allow the double-height chapter room to completely open itself to the courtyard and serve as a stage to small events taking place within each house. Rolling screens open each sorority's courtyard to the pedestrian street and lawn areas for larger social and academic functions.

This housing complex seamlessly joins student living, learning, and playing with the Sonoran desert environment. Each courtyard incorporates native trees and plantings that provide shade during warm summer months and solar access during cooler months. Visible through the semi-transparent rolling screens, this landscape spills out of each individual courtyard and into the community, creating shaded outdoor spaces for student interaction.

2

1. The complex is a village of forms that provide cohesiveness and distinct spaces for each sorority group. 2. There are 12 courtyard houses for 400 students. Common courtyards can be used for large social events. 3. The colors and forms compose a soothing desert aesthetic, a good fit for the Arizona campus. 4. An airy common study area is bright with daylight. 5. Private courtyards serve as outdoor rooms during temperate months.

3

4

First Covenant Church
Salina, Kansas

SOCIAL HUB FOR A FAITH COMMUNITY   The growing First Covenant Church needed a new building in which to worship and gather. A four-day charrette led to a design that stressed the congregation's emphasis on social space— this faith community believes that the church is for individual spirituality and for group interaction—and their desire to make a visible statement in the community on their hilly site.

The site and the central Kansas geology—a landscape of carved valleys known as the Flint Hills—became an inspiration for the project. The project comprises large forms arrayed on the ridge of one of the highest hills in Salina. Abstractly, they are forms of the landscape, replicating its scale and using it to denote sacred ground. There are two formal forces at work: a horizontal mass that has the sense of growing out of the earth and a vertical mass that marks the threshold of the church. The mixture of these powerful dynamics is the central design statement of this project.

The congregation needed larger, more flexible worship space and a comfortable, beautiful space for interaction before and after services. The old facility had an insufficient and poorly lit lobby space; church members wanted an identifiable entry and commodious community gathering space. The result was a spacious foyer that is an important hub of the facility and visible throughout the city below.

The key spaces of the project—foyer, fellowship hall, and sanctuary—respond to the site by taking advantage of the key views to the west. Formally, these spaces rise above the horizon with large, pitched roofs that loom over the landscape. The roofs are detailed in a similar manner that literally meets the building committee's desire for a congregation under "one roof." The education and administration spaces take a secondary role, both in the church community and in the orientation on the site. These secondary spaces are more homogenous than the gathering spaces, and are grouped under the same single-story parapet with little discernment between the education and administrative spaces.

The sanctuary space was designed to be flexible; the floor is flat and chairs are not fixed. It is a simple space, lightly adorned; the clean aesthetic is successful because detailing has been handled with care. Throughout the project, materials express an honest clarity appropriate to the project budget and the congregation's desire for a statement without pretense.

1. The new church on a rural site has a dramatic central volume and contrasting skin materials. 2. The prairie setting and central Kansas landforms inspired the design. 3. The stylized cross in the main lobby volume is visible from both inside and outside the space. 4. The cylindrical central volume is positioned at the intersection of two angular volumes. 5. The sanctuary space occupies one of the angular volumes. The space is enlivened by varied ceiling planes and lighting.

4

5

College of Business Administration
Tampa, Florida

EXPANDED COLLEGE, FRESH IMAGE The University of South Florida's College of Business Administration is a 45,500-square-foot addition to a late 1970s energy efficient building—an earth-integrated campus icon. The addition creates a new, corporate-yet-academic image for the College of Business. The addition is targeted toward graduate and executive graduate programs and is also meant for use as a social setting and new entry portal for the school.

The new facility includes a 6,000-square-foot atrium—the new center of the school, eight new classrooms that serve 50 people each, a new dean's suite, a corporate board room, and multi-purpose dining space and auditorium that will be focused toward after hour activities.

These elements of the program are arranged to help further reinforce the development of a linear bar of function and circulation and respect the powerful geometry of the existing school. The ensuing linear façade along the school's main north/south street enables the new facility to engage the public. This façade is a new, clear identity for the school.

Connecting to the existing building posed a unique challenge due to the 20-foot tall earth berm that surrounds the facility. To create a harmonious link between old and new, the eastern portion of the berm was removed, leaving the remaining shared space between facilities open to the public. This newly created outdoor area is a commodious courtyard complement to the indoor atrium space—together they are a nexus and new main entry to the school.

In keeping with the energy consciousness of the existing facility, the new building utilizes vertical extension devices for shading. The pattern created by these shading devices alludes to gears and creates a sensation of the linear elements in motion. This sensation is a prelude to the expected future growth of the school, which would take place to the north or south.

2

3

1. The building is the college's new front door; a glass wall heightens connections between the lobby and campus. 2. The lobby/atrium is the new hub of the college and a spacious setting for social gatherings. A floating steel stairway is the centerpiece of the glass-walled lobby. 3. Most classrooms have a wall of windows for daylight and views to the campus setting. 4. The addition to the business college has given it a new identity on campus. Great care was taken to preserve existing mature trees on the site.

Eccles Center for Performing Arts & Horne School of Music

Ephraim, Utah

SOUNDSCAPE The George S. and Dolores Doré Eccles Center for the Performing Arts & Horne School of Music at Snow College are two departments with unique identities, music and theater, housed in one building. This is a learning environment where the play, and the playing of instruments, is the thing. The challenge was to scale down the volume required for the reverberation of each of the performance halls. The performance spaces are evident in the dark masses. Classrooms surround the dark masses, punctuating the space with undulating windows that read as a musical score. Color and change in plane create relief in the façade by articulating the masonry. Light and shadow further animate the façade, framing fragments of instruments and students from the outside and framing the mountains and landscape from within. Benches are cast into the masonry and aluminum shrouds frame the windows. Along with window boxes, these benches are inhabited by students to create a "living wall" that further mediates scale.

The two distinct programs are linked in the lobby with a ceiling plane that takes the form of a knot. The knot is composed of two colors of fabric fused between two layers of Knoll-manufactured transparent acrylic, called Imago. This ceiling installation is the largest installation of Imago in the world. The material is transparent when lit from above and opaque when lit from below. The dramatic form sets the stage for the lobby on performance nights, as a place to see and be seen.

The ceiling plane of the concert hall performance space is a soundscape that manipulates sound by transforming the space that it inhabits—and thus requires manipulating the space for maximum acoustical performance. The focus in the concert hall is the stage. Typically, the orchestra shell is a blond wood, like maple, in order to contrast with the mahogany wood of the instruments as well as the formal black attire of the performers. The orchestra shell is sound reflective and extends into the house as sound louvers. The volume of the concert hall is utilized as a reverberant cavity. The maple-colored soundscape ribbon in the concert hall is reflective at the stage and transparent over the house. The seats and the floor plane are the same color. Together, the forms, materials, and colors create the soundscape of the concert hall.

3

1. Staggered planes punched with metal-framed glazing give the building a readable façade. 2. The two parts of the buildings are knotted in the dramatic central lobby using "ribbons" that extend from the concert hall and the theater. The sketch is a soundscape diagram that informed the parti.
3. Metal-framed window boxes offer passersby glimpses of practicing thespians and musicians inside, making the building's face a kind of "living wall."
4. The 720-seat concert hall is surrounded by classrooms and office space. The light, transparent ceiling planes in the hall become the ribbon leading to the knot—the metaphor for uniting dual programs in the building— in the lobby.

4

Grandview Community Center
Grandview, Missouri

1

A PEOPLE PLACE IN THE PARK The City of Grandview, an established small community within the Kansas City metropolitan area, was looking to reinforce its strong sense of community with a new community center. The desire was to create a community-wide magnet, in the form of a 60,000-square-foot multi-use facility, within an undeveloped area of existing Meadowmere park. Gould Evans collaborated with Ankeny Kell Architects on this project, now called "The View."

The site has a gentle slope from north to south and a grove of trees at the north of the property. The building's L shape responds to the position of the grove, while its orientation allows people to experience a connection to the site from several areas within the structure. The grove was an important site amenity and featured prominently in discussions about the project from the outset, including during the community design workshop, ultimately becoming its guiding metaphor.

The building is organized along a central corridor with visual connections between outdoor and indoor public spaces. An upper-level entry provides views into aquatics and the gymnasium below. Other components include new office space for the Parks and Recreation Department, childcare drop-off, fitness areas, elevated walk/jog track, rock climbing wall, senior room, craft room, support spaces, and a banquet/multipurpose space for up to 250 people. The multipurpose wing for functions wraps the grove. Pre-function space is outfitted with track lighting and a concealed art display track. Interior spaces are flooded with natural light from large windows. Light monitors in the central corridor have patterned glazing that filters luminosity, creating ever-changing patterns throughout the space. There are other subtle nods to the trees as a driving metaphor, including the steel columns in the main hall and the slender, angled, wood-wrapped columns at the building's exterior overhangs. The many windows that let in light during the day give the building a transparency and glow at night.

Light monitors serve as beacons for this public building and as anchors of the main hall inside; they are positioned at the hubs—the front desk and threshold of the social wing. As visitors enter the center from either end of the building, they experience a wash of filtered light from above. Moving through the hall, they have an eye-level outlook to the trees along with views through the interior spaces out onto the park. The result is a memorable place in this new center of the community.

2

3

4

1. Dancing columns and a glowing light monitor give the community center a lively, vibrant presence. 2. The center will host activities day and night; the notion of having a beacon-like illumination was important. 3. Etched glass filters daylight in a leafy pattern, referencing the center's park setting and the importance of the connection to the outdoors. 4. The airy central space is the building's hub. 5. The center includes a swimming pool, gymnasium, craft areas, and many flexible meeting spaces; it serves numerous age groups.

5

The Biodesign Institute
Tempe, Arizona

A PLACE FOR FORWARD-LOOKING RESEARCH The Biodesign Institute is a state-of-the-art research facility that houses the vanguard of contemporary science, bridging across disciplines—industry, government, and academia. Located on the Tempe campus of Arizona State University, the institute is dedicated to interdisciplinary research and the collaborative partnerships of biotechnology, nanotechnology, and information technology. Building A is a $73 million, 172,000-square-foot facility that opened in Fall 2004, while Building B opened in Fall 2005. The facility was a collaborative design effort between Gould Evans and Lord, Aeck & Sargent.

Interdisciplinary research is at the heart of the institute's strategy and also serves as the inspiration for the building design to enhance the value, mission, and culture of the institute. The values of communication, collaboration, and connection reverberate through the open, light-filled atrium and laboratories. Together, these principals meet the call for high-tech, flexible research space that is designed for permanence while providing an aesthetic that is open, beautiful, and inspiring.

The architecture team approached the design using these organizing principals, in order to encourage communication and collaboration at every level—between buildings, between floors, between the university and the community—fostering individual success as well as technology transfer among researchers.

Through extensive research and case study analysis, the design team devised a concept for the building's organization that encourages both planned and informal communication among researchers. The lab, office, and conference spaces converge around an open atrium that links people visually, vertically, and horizontally in the four-story building—maximizing collaboration and interaction among researchers.

For a facility that delves into the mystery of nature, it was important that the building design maintain a connection to natural light, materials, and the outside. The building rises from a large, beautifully landscaped Sonoran desert garden located in the forecourt. The development of the garden and the open space in the plan create a sense of presence and world-class image for the entire complex. Additionally, the ceilings within the building are held as high as possible, with glass partitions to the exterior, permitting views to the outside from deep in the lab spaces, so that researchers can see the treetops and be connected to the natural rhythms of the day.

1

1. The large building reads as a strong yet elegant masonry form. 2. The glazing is shaded by a metal scrim that suggests shifting planes and indeterminate mass. 3.This use of metal lightens the masonry volume and affords interior spaces views and light without glare. 4. Interdisciplinary work is encouraged by open circulation spaces and the copious use of glass for transparency throughout.

2

5. The central atrium is topped with a long skylight at the spine of the building; this airy core is part of an overall strategy of transparency, visibility, and openness. 6. Contrasting materials and careful detailing contribute to a distinctive building skin. 7. The ground floor lounge space is bounded by floor-to-ceiling glass; it was important that views to the campus outside be preserved, and that the building appear open and welcoming to passersby. 8. The building appears to glow behind its shading screen.

6

7

8

Baron BMW
Merriam, Kansas

THE PLAY OF DISPLAY For this project, the challenge was to create a new kind of auto dealership that includes a showroom reflective of the engineering quality of the auto manufacturer, comprising a naturally ventilated service area with 22 service bays, an administration area, training facilities, and underground car storage. The steeply sloped site is at one of the highest elevations in the area, at the intersection of two major traffic arteries.

Reinventing the building type was made possible through introducing a sense of play and movement. The resulting concept displays the vehicles in a series of salons rather than one big room. Each salon is sized to accommodate just a few cars, allowing the customer to be hosted in a comfortably scaled, low-pressure environment.

The design started with one of the auto manufacturer's trademark showroom features, a roadway delineated into the showroom floor with cars arrayed along it. Here, the road was curved and then transformed into a ramp. The ramp design allows visitors a gentle passage between the three main levels and into the different salons, viewing cars along the way. This concept effectively utilizes the natural grades of the site, creates a "continuum of experiences" focused on the products, and enhances sales.

Floor depths are minimized to maintain openness and visibility across the showroom. A central strut provides clerestory light to the primary sales salons. Leather-wrapped handrails, pear wood millwork, and careful detailing reflect the high-quality product. White porcelain cladding defines the primary sales areas.

The service area and the remainder of the building envelope are faced with silver metal panels to reflect their supporting role. Service bays are stacked to provide for teaming of specialists. Glass exterior garage doors, clerestory light, operable windows, and ceiling fans provide natural ventilation. While light colored epoxy flooring creates an open, airy work environment for the service technicians.

3

4

1. Glass jewel boxes arrayed along an interior ramp feature the cars and protrude from the white cylindrical forms, lighting up the exterior façade. 2-3. The glass boxes give the building visibility from nearby roadways and provide a sense of "peeking in" on the luxury cars on view inside; they also bring light to the interior spaces. 4. Clerestory windows bring natural light to the showroom floor, where customers consult in single-car "salons" with company representatives.

Rinker Hall
School of Building Construction
Gainesville, Florida

RAISING THE BAR ON PERFORMANCE M.E. Rinker Sr. Hall accommodates 450 students on three levels. The program called for classrooms, teaching labs, construction labs, offices, and other facilities. In a joint venture with Croxton Collaborative, Gould Evans design teams engaged in charrettes that included campus administration, faculty, and students of the Schools of Architecture and Building Construction. This project has been LEED certified at the Gold level by the U.S. Green Building Council.

The building became a "rock in the stream" of student pathways. Large live oaks and a student gathering spot under the trees were protected. The site could have accommodated the program in a two-story structure, but the team designed three stories to minimize site footprint and provide for more vegetated areas and open space. Organized on a north/south solar axis to maximize deep daylighting, the project utilized DOE 2.2 (energy) and Superlite 2.0 (daylighting) analyses to optimize the balance of natural and built systems. From the central public stair and daylight-washed atrium to classrooms with large exterior windows, shaped ceiling geometries, and deep daylighting louvers, the building is dramatically illuminated by daylight. Exposed circulation and structural and mechanical systems allow students to interpret the building as a whole.

A major design challenge arose when basic building science demanded a glass and metal building envelope to release heat quickly, while the campus context called for a brick masonry exterior wall (heat retention). The resolution is a metal and glass building with a free-standing masonry shading wall on west and south to address heavier thermal loads at these exposures. Utilizing masonry at these most public elevations answered the need for a building that performs and belongs. High performance attributes have resulted in a building with 56 percent energy savings above ASHRAE 90.1/1999, customized daylighting, and an exterior wall system carefully designed to balance moisture, thermal loading and daylight, while ensuring long life and low maintenance.

Rinker Hall demonstrates that a LEED Gold building can be constructed within market costs; it was completed at $170 per square foot. This was the first Florida building designed using LEED; the campus has since adopted LEED Silver as a minimum standard.

1

1. A brick wall responds to campus context; it stands in front of the façade and provides shade and thermal updraft. 2. Skylights and a large, airy, ceiling-glazed atrium spine are some of the key elements drawing light through the circulation spaces. 3. A major accomplishment at Rinker Hall was orienting the building on a pure north-south axis without compromising full-spectrum light or creating a glare problem. 4. Driving the daylight approach was the notion that learning environments enlivened by variation of light intensity, color, and direction as the day passes are healthier and support higher productivity.

Johnson County Library
Blue Valley
Overland Park, Kansas

ENLIGHTENED ENVIRONMENT   The library is the second component of a planned community center development in a growing suburb of Kansas City. The district the library serves is populated by professionals and families that have located to the area within the last ten years. In addition to the library, the community development includes an elementary school, community center, pool structure, walking trails, park, and shared parking.

The goal was to create a 25,000-square-foot library with patron-friendly features such as a full-service drive-up window, drive-up book return, café, public meeting room, art gallery, collections, and electronic resources. The program required maximum sightlines from staffing positions while maintaining the necessary acoustic separation between public service areas.

The design for the new library is based on movement— the movement of patrons as they converge across the wide approaches to the site; the movement of vehicles to access a service window; the movement of materials through the site and building; and the movement of light that traces the arc of the building all through the day.

The program demanded interaction between patrons in vehicles and the building itself, and this was achieved through a design concept that involves the rotation of space and planes around a centrally focused courtyard. Inside, curving walls lead patrons through the library as a boulevard with multiple opportunities along the route. The clerestory window band allows tight, moving beams of light to rake across the floor and walls that frame the central boulevard space, providing a constant reminder of the traverse of the day. The ends of the boulevard are both glass. The central courtyard is viewed through floor-to-ceiling glass and changes colors throughout the day as the sun moves from south to east. Horizontal, perforated sunshades shade the glass. This is a light-infused learning environment.

The courtyard features a rock garden, seating, a butterfly garden, xeriscape plantings, and coniferous and deciduous trees. This oasis is visible from all the primary interior rooms in the building and functions as an extension of those interior spaces, into which it brings filtered natural light.

1. A curving masonry wall and cantilever define the entry of the library. 2. The curved shape of the building is reflected in a curved circulation path. 3. The shaded courtyard brings filtered light and views to reading areas. 4. The curve of the building defines the interior spaces. 5. At night, window walls glow with light. 6. The low-scale library has an approachable feel and complements its residential neighborhood.

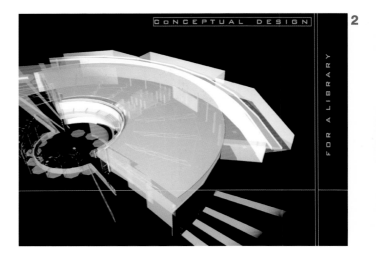

5

Pearson Hall
School of Education
Lawrence, Kansas

NEW HOME FOR TEACHING PROGRAM The University of Kansas chose to renovate a seven-story, 1950s-era residence hall for use as the new home for the School of Education. To accommodate more than 300 offices and 30 teaching spaces, an addition of 30,000 square feet was required.

Located on the western edge of the main campus, Joseph R. Pearson Hall overlooks scenic Potter's Lake, and commands a sweeping view of the campus, known as the Hill, and its Kansas landscape. This location, however, was perceived as remote from the main campus by many of the project's user groups. Staff and faculty were concerned about the idea of occupying what they saw as an old dorm. The dean envisioned a building with strong character that would represent the newly reorganized School of Education, which has a strong reputation in the region and the country.

New construction was planned for two locations in order to maximize the transformation. A five-story addition at the west entrance provides office and seminar spaces and refreshes the building's west façade. Located on the east side, the larger, two-story addition houses classroom, lab, and lecture space, and provides a new entrance lobby and student commons. Brick cladding complements the existing building's skin. Metal panel emulates, without mimicking, existing limestone. The southern portion of the east addition was rotated to create a large opening at the center. This is the commons and east entry; expansive views of the campus serve as an important visual orientation tool. The circulation spine at each level culminates with a view out from this opening.

The east and west glass-walled entries are connected by wide, open stairs inside the central spine. A large skylight accentuates this circulation spine. Floor patterns and exterior paving patterns are coordinated to flow from exterior to interior, creating another level of connection between inside and out. Along the main circulation spine is the Instructional Technology Lab, which showcases resources and materials in use by the school's students. A complete renovation of the seven-story tower involved removing the existing modular window system and revamping the dormitory layout. The new floor plan effectively "de-dorms" the corridor system. Large open spaces break up the long wings, flooding the corridor with light. At the exterior, a new, dynamic window pattern ties the existing building to the additions, and transforms the old building into a modern campus structure.

1. The addition of 30,000 square feet helped transform an old residence hall into a state-of-the-art teaching and learning environment for a leading school of education. 2. The large, airy lobby also functions as a student commons. 3.The glass wall marks the lobby entrance and glows from within at night. 4. The addition is located in new volumes, which create new entries on both sides of the building. 5. A grand stair in the lobby was necessary because of the site's steep grade, but the design team turned it into an opportunity for a dramatic focal point.

First United Methodist Church
Blue Springs, Missouri

QUIET QUALITY The physical program for this project called for a 550-seat sanctuary, music rehearsal space, child development spaces, and classrooms. This is the first of several phases; the worship space will eventually serve as the grand narthex and fellowship hall to a future, much larger sanctuary. The site is planned for a columbarium, large and open play fields, a maintenance facility, a small pond, meditation gardens, an outdoor worship area, an outdoor amphitheater, and parking for up to 700 cars.

The First United Methodist Church congregation acquired a former 22-acre farmstead near Lake Tapawingo for their new facilities and growing congregation. Using a consensus building process based on a series of "town hall" congregation meetings, a dramatic and realistic concept for the master plan was developed. The master plan for the site articulates a strong interplay between the natural features of the rolling site and the desire for an inspiring, sacred awareness in form.

The sanctuary is set back from the street and located on the high point of the site with large windows on the east face serving as a beacon at night. The building will expand into a village of structures stepping down the hill and framing a central courtyard. A simple rock and water baptismal font sits beneath an east-facing window on axis with a pond to the west. The sanctuary opens to the west with views of the landscape and the pond. Classrooms and narthex spaces flank the sanctuary and create an outdoor worship space.

The entrance to the narthex lobby is a semi-circular masonry arc, a focal point for worshippers. The sanctuary is a simple shed form that rises to the east. The western edge of the sanctuary is a pedestrian-scaled colonnade with floor-to-ceiling glass providing views of the worship gardens and the worship trail. The east edge of the sanctuary has a continuous band of clerestory glass, shaded with vertical wood louvers and controlled with a deep interior soffit to wash light along the inside wall. Detailing demonstrates a craft-based functionalism and responds to a modest budget.

The ceiling graduates in height toward a primary vault above the chancel. Three wood-wrapped bays, opening to the south, allow traces of light to move across the floor toward the chancel. These three openings are placeholders for future access to the ultimate, permanent worship space.

1. Careful detailing of simple materials resulted in a well-crafted building for this congregation. 2. Metal canopies line the edge of the sanctuary. 3. These provide a shaded edge for the courtyard. 4. The stonework gives the sanctuary a solid, sturdy aesthetic that also has a soft, natural feel.

3

4

Athletes' Performance Institute
Tempe, Arizona

SPORTS BY DESIGN Situated within a prominent sports corridor on the Arizona State University campus, the Athletes' Performance Institute is a comprehensive, world-class facility devoted to the training of professional and amateur athletes. The 30,000-square-foot facility seamlessly integrates the activities of athletes, elite level coaches, sport scientists, and sport therapists dedicated to optimizing athletic performance.

The complex is organized as a linear north-facing bar emphasizing indoor/outdoor flexibility. An extension of the roof structure to the north creates a steel canopy that acts as a protective brim to shield athletes from the elements. The indoor/outdoor threshold at this zone is further dissolved by the use of glazed overhead doors, retracting as climate permits, for warm-up and stretching. The site strategy enhances the athletes' experiences through visibility of the training/swimming pool, sprint track, and synthetic/turf field. The athletic field zone is engaged by a 220-foot-long, 12-foot-tall, freestanding concrete wall that focuses on a variety of intensive one-on-one training exercises.

The interior design for the facility depicts zones that are designated for training (work) and rejuvenation (rest). The work area consists of a fully equipped weight room, and exam and evaluation rooms. The rest area includes men's and women's locker rooms, and a rehabilitation area including a hot/cold plunge, underwater treadmill, multipurpose theater space, and nutrition bar. The two primary zones are connected by a centrally located athletic hall of fame gallery that doubles as an entry lobby and transition zone.

The building design is a tribute to the human body. Structural steel is analogous to the body's bone structure, held together by variable masses (muscle) and covered by layers of glass representing skin. Project materials—exposed steel, glass, sand-blasted concrete block, and corrugated metal all converge to reveal a straightforward modern architectural aesthetic that embraces the dynamic qualities of sport, and captures the client's goal of being true to the athlete.

2

3

1. Garage-style doors open in temperate weather; the building essentially recedes, leaving the workout room open to the track and pool outdoors. 2. Offices are adjacent to the lobby, the social hub of the building, which also includes a Hall of Fame gallery. 3. The entry façade has a modest, clean-lined profile; simple masonry plans are broken up by fenestration slots. 4. The training facility extends onto the grounds where a pool and soaking tub are elegantly recessed.

Cedar City Public Library
Cedar City, Utah

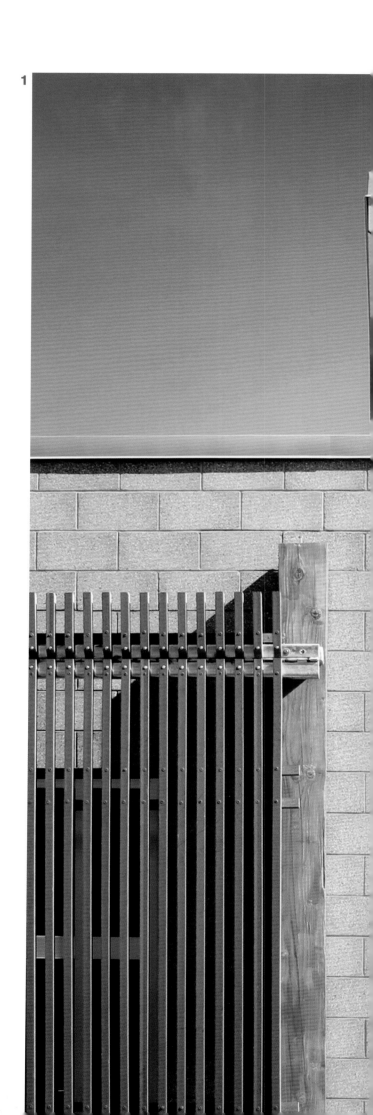

LIBRARY IN THE PARK Interactive workshops were used to unearth the needs and shared goals for the library; these sessions involved library staff, library board, the mayor, city council members, Friends of the Library, Southern Utah University representatives, and community members. The concept that evolved from these workshops was the library in a park. Linking the new library with an important public open space is intended to make the library a community catalyst to encourage lifelong learning including leisure reading, education, literacy, community, and cultural activities.

The library leaders were interested in a natural aesthetic—drawing on the park location and an interest in sustainable design measures—and they wanted a sophisticated, state-of-the-art facility. This presented the opportunity for the design team to create an architectural language that involved natural and manmade materials. The composite impression is tactile and natural, but refined and elegant. Heavy timber structural elements (salvaged from the Great Salt Lake railroad trestle) are exposed; this provides a contrast with the elegant cherry benches and casework.

The floor, at the perimeter of the general collection area and at circulation, is exposed, polished concrete. This continues out into the landscape of the park outside to create a series of reading terraces. A glass wall helps dissolve the physical boundary between the building and its park site.

The internal geometries of the structure are simple and rectangular, except at the public interface areas, where lines become rounded and softened. The entry façade, which faces east along the path from the parking lot to the park, is a broad, sweeping curve clad in red sandstone, a reference to the red hills for which Cedar City is known.

The masonry was laid in curved forms at the exterior to define exterior spaces, just as it was used to create rooms at the interior. Individual blocks of masonry were turned at a right angle to the wall at window openings to create deep shadows adding more definition to the smooth wall surface. Special block shapes were created to permit this creative expression (to the library board, this was also a fund-raising opportunity: at the interior gallery wall, the masonry was engraved with the names of library donors). At the southwest corner of the building, a sunscreen filters the light and heat while allowing views to the city park.

3

4

5

6

1. Simplicity and contrast were two of the driving themes for this library. 2. Uplighting on the masonry wall at night creates a dramatic look. 3. A wall of windows is welcoming and provides views into the park. 4. Careful detailing lends modest materials elegance and precision.
5. The simple interior space includes casual reading areas along a window wall. 6. At night, the window wall is a beacon of light in the park.

East Campus Student Union
Mesa, Arizona

1

STUDENT NEXUS   The new Student Union at Arizona State University's East Campus, a former military base, is now an epicenter of student activity. The building acts as a hub of campus life facilitating social interaction among students, faculty, and the community. Opened in the fall of 2004, the union provides a vibrant new image for the rapidly growing campus.

The building acts as a container of activity with large multi-functional and flexible spaces that open up to a future pedestrian mall and plaza space. The south portion houses a student lounge and dining area that open on three sides to outdoor patios and the main central circulation area. This space includes a coffee shop, game room, information desk, and bookstore. The 400-seat banquet hall opens to an exterior lobby and formal lawn area used for gatherings.

There is a direct relationship between the surrounding agricultural environment and the building design. The ceiling inside the large open dining/lounge space mimics the rows found in adjacent fields. An exterior dining canopy supported by steel beams continues the connection from inside to outside to future pedestrian paths and indigenous desert landscaping. The linear movement throughout the building resembles driving past rolling agricultural fields.

Expansive glass walls, carefully shaded to prevent direct sunlight from entering the building, invite students into the union with generous views of the activity inside. Large overhead garage-type doors connect the interior and shaded exterior dining areas. The bookstore, located in the main entry, also includes an overhead door that can be opened for outdoor patio sales.

The design respects the relationship between a polytechnic campus and natural desert environment. The building shell is covered in a corrugated metal scrim and painted deep red to recall brick buildings of older, more established university campuses and the colors of the Sonoran Desert. The outer building envelope is offset from the scrim to provide shaded walkways around the building and shading for interior spaces. The scrim reduces direct sunlight by 70 percent, allowing the building to operate more efficiently.

1. This is the first new building on the East Campus, which occupies the site (and several buildings) of a former military base. 2. Steel frames mark the courtyard and entry of the union; steel scrims shade the heavily glazed walls. 3. Angular ceiling planes add visual interest in the main student commons, which benefits from daylight and views to the campus beyond. 4. The bookstore occupies one corner of the building and opens to the common space. 5. Around the perimeter of the building, there are pockets of seating.

2

4

3

5

Love of Christ Lutheran Church
Mesa, Arizona

MULTI-USE MAXIMIZED The Love of Christ Lutheran Church takes the notion of multipurpose to new heights. The 22,000-square-foot facility program called for a 1,000-seat, state-of-the-art contemporary worship space as well as a space for recreational sports and performance.

This unique mix of functions posed many inherent challenges to the design team. The new building needed to respect the scale of existing traditional buildings while satisfying the height requirements of a basketball court. It had to create intimate spaces for worship as well as provide flexible and functional spaces for recreation sports such as basketball. The material palette had to be durable to withstand high impact recreational use, while also having the acoustical and visual appeal for a dignified worship environment.

The design solution reveals these dualities. The overall form takes cues from the surrounding mountain landscape and reads as a low-rise cluster of solid masses nestled into its desert site. It extends the orthogonal grid of the existing building, unites the existing campus around a new central courtyard, and projects a sense of outreach to the greater community. From the exterior, the building's most identifying feature is a leaning wall that shears across the site like a geologic fault line to split and raise the building's mass towards the street.

The multi-use space is organized around two intersecting axes. The interior of the space parallels the axis of the existing building and is delicately shaped for necessary acoustical reflection and proper sight-lines. Major public zones are concealed behind a perforated screen wall with accent lighting that shines at night to passersby. The building merges body and soul together in a response that speaks of its time and place.

SALT Center
Tucson, Arizona

LEARNING CENTER The Strategic Alternatives Learning Techniques (SALT) Center at the University of Arizona provides services to students with learning disabilities and furnishes support to learning disabilities research and community outreach programs. The vision for this nationally recognized program was to provide a series of concentrated learning atmospheres within an intimate yet public environment focused on supporting a culturally diverse community of learners.

The SALT Center is located on the north edge of the campus bordering a residential district and busy pedestrian thoroughfare. This meant that the building had to be both an urban neighborhood building and a campus building. The red brick masonry ties the building to the campus. Along the active campus edge, spatial carvings and projections reveal and conceal movement within the building. The ground floor recedes to create the entry into the building. A breezeway frames the courtyard, which sets the tone as a flexible environment—a stage for learning and communication—that continues throughout the building.

The facility provides interior and exterior spaces that can be utilized for multiple functions while providing flexibility for future modifications to support the evolving nature of the program and instructional technologies. The 16,000-square-foot, three-story building includes instructional offices, computer laboratories with assisted learning technologies, tutorial spaces, meeting rooms with interactive technology, and a lounge.

The design provides the SALT Center with an interactive arrangement of spaces that reinforces interdisciplinary activities within the program. This intimate courtyard located at the heart of the building is the catalyst for academic and social exchange. The outdoor space shaded by indigenous desert landscape serves as the destination for faculty and students crossing paths.

1. The notched brick and punched windows give the simple mass a rhythmic façade. The SALT Center occupies a highly visible corner of campus that is also a heavy pedestrian passageway. 2. An internal courtyard provides important access to light, air, and vegetations. 3. A perforated metal scrim provides shade but allows views from a wall of windows. 4. Learning spaces benefit from natural light. 5. The entry lobby is a transparent volume at the ground floor beneath the brick volume which appears to float above.

3

4

5

BleuJacket
Lawrence, Kansas

THE FRENCH CURVE An 1863 grain storage building was used to showcase the contemporary detailing for a sophisticated new restaurant. The goal of the design was to create a balance between the exposed, rectilinear limestone walls and timber beams of the existing structure and the softly sinuous shapes of the new space, including the sweeping French curve ramp (which also satisfies ADA requirements).

The designers chose an elegantly restrained pallet of materials to strike an elemental balance of opposing forces: of the contemporary sophistication versus the rustic historic stone and timber structure; the playful, curvilinear new elements versus the rectilinear space; and the lightness of the drapery versus the solidity of the building elements.

Design details include overstuffed seating, leather-wrapped handrails, iridescent upholstery, and drapery—both moiré opaque and shimmering gold transparent—which separates space and curves seductively around the dining areas and oval booths. In some booths, the occupants can achieve complete privacy.

Low-voltage lighting is programmed to be flexible, highlighting the layers of space and flattering the diners and the food. Every effort was made to avoid overhead equipment and obstruction. The overall effect is rich with visual interest.

The lighting design concepts were derived to provide highlights and sparkle in a low ambient setting and to let the light, rather than the fixtures, be the statement so that the focus is on the beauty of the food and the diners.

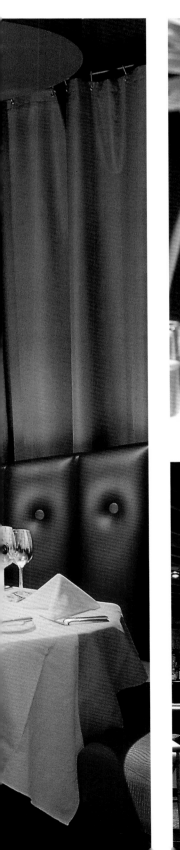

St. Paul's United Methodist Church

Lenexa, Kansas

NATURAL ADDITION The congregation of St. Paul's United Methodist Church in Lenexa, Kansas, asked the Gould Evans architects to turn their church into a functional place of worship that capitalizes on the natural beauty of the surrounding woods. The dramatic 14-acre setting for St. Paul's current church and new addition contains a wooded creek and small pond, and includes plenty of space for a growing congregation.

The first-phase addition, which was completed in the fall of 2004, includes classroom and administrative space as well as a bridge to connect the existing building to the future sanctuary that will be located across the creek. The prominent new addition, coupled with the enhancement of the natural site features, creates a new identity for St. Paul's and enhances the church's co-existence with the landscape.

The bridge, supported by wood timbers and cross-bracing, is defined by a large curving wall of naturally weathered redwood, that continues to sweep up and grow in elevation as it crosses the stream. The wall symbolizes outreach and growth—quietly foreshadowing the future sanctuary. The space along the bridge creates a strong connection to nature through its use of natural materials, exposed wood structure, and extensive glazing. The classrooms have a tree house-like feel, as they project from the bridge, overlooking the stream below.

There is a playful articulation of windows along the eastern wall, which relates to the dappled light shining through the surrounding trees. The openings progress from small to large as they approach the culmination of the bridge on the other side of the stream—another indication of the future growth of the congregation. The west-facing windows open up to the pools and stream with large expanses of glass.

Between the classrooms and high above the creek is a deck where church members can reflect on their faith, amidst the sights and sounds of nature. Grant funding will make it possible to utilize native wetland plants and limestone rock found on site to filter storm water runoff through the site, making this one of the "greenest" places in the surrounding area.

2

3

1. The new church facility is built on a wooded site with dramatic elevation changes and a creek and pond. 2. The pattern of fenestration helps create a sense of dynamism and movement in the classroom wing. 3. The windows bring light and views to the spaces inside and enliven the building's façade. 4. The end of the classroom wing is supported on pylons, allowing it to stretch over the creek and lending the rooms a treehouse feel.

4

Arts & Technology Complex
Overland Park, Kansas

HIGH-TECH HUMANISM The Arts & Technology Complex at the Johnson County Community College will be comprised of the Regnier Center for Technology & Business, by Gould Evans, and the Nerman Museum of Contemporary Art, by Kyu Sung Woo Architects. The 150,000-square-foot technology center will house classrooms and offices for Bio Sciences, Continuing Education, Computer Information Systems, and Information Support Services. The museum includes galleries, a café, auditorium, classrooms, and offices. The College's mission was to create a preeminent technology and arts complex that blends with the campus and demonstrates how both art and technology can be meaningful enrichments in daily lives.

Both buildings are inspired by the existing campus typology—heavily grounded masonry buildings with rigorous patterns of deep fenestration and two- and three-story massing. But they both uproot this static context with a dynamic relationship between ground plane and interior. The west garden pavilion of the technology center weaves the surrounding courtyards through its colonnades. As the building extends east, masonry planes disconnect from the ground plane, suggesting a levitative quality over sub-grade parking. The museum's solid upper galleries, clad in limestone, seem to hover over the glass lobby. The tension alludes to an unseen advancement in technology, inherent within the buildings' construction systems.

The complex will be an inviting, transparent gateway into this formerly introverted 1960s campus. At the juncture of the buildings, a transparent atrium serves as a centerpiece to the complex, lobby, and events hall. New media art installations in this link are extended into the Regnier Center lobby and public spaces, culminating with a projection scrim over the southern entrance. Media installations activate the solar film on this two story glazed volume, which is also a demonstration lab for emerging technologies.

The complex cultivates a strong connection to the natural environment by utilizing natural materials such as limestone and wood and optimizing daylight and views. Warm interior spaces include a diverse range of spaces for learning, socializing, and display. High-performance building features include optimized energy systems, enhanced indoor air quality, low-flow plumbing fixtures, recycled-content materials, automated lighting control systems, and a high-performance building envelope. The site design increases available green space (via underground parking), reduces storm water runoff, and minimizes light pollution.

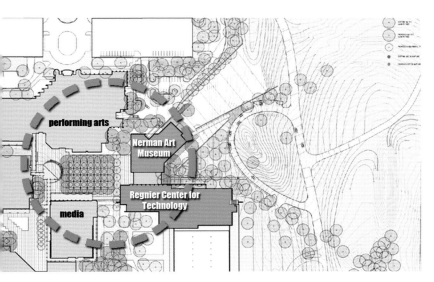

performing arts

Nerman Art Museum

Regnier Center for Technology

media

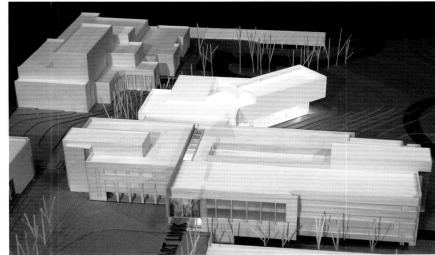

Indian Creek Community Church
Overland Park, Kansas

existing building

COMMUNITY SPIRIT After nearly ten years of worshiping in a fellowship hall, the Indian Creek Community Church congregation is nearing completion of their master plan's final phase. This phase calls for a 1,200-seat sanctuary, hospitality space, lobby, administrative offices, adult and youth classrooms, and other youth play spaces to meet the future needs of a growing congregation. The designers' challenge was to design an addition that more than doubles the size of the church and allows for the logical arrangement of spaces while resulting in a cohesive whole.

This new elements are designed to fit with the existing building. Beyond just copying color, material, and detail of the existing building, the design has an informality that matches the spirit of the existing one in form and relates to the wide range of life activities that take place here.

The sanctuary remains the most significant place in the life of the church; it is the key symbolic form expressing gathering, worship, and community for the faithful. The sanctuary addresses the church's desire to have an awareness of God's creation, and a theatrical environment that suits this faith community's services. The sanctuary is composed of an inner skin rendered in cherry wood and an outer skin (both roof and walls) clad in zinc metal.

The design places the new functional elements along the edge of the existing functions. The primary circulation path for the entire church will stitch the two together in a seam that connects, lightens, and conveys the spirit of activity and the importance of this as a gathering place. The lobby becomes an interstitial space, one in between old and new. Monolithic stone flooring provides the foundation for accommodating the church's desire to connect and unify in a casual and informal manner. The path of this seam forms a center; the symbolic place where the teaching of the Bible connects with everyday life. Building on the queue of new spaces, the lobby swells to signify a heart from which many spaces can be accessed.

The hospitality room, prayer room, and courtyard with baptismal pool play a significant role in the daily life of the church. These spaces create an inward-focused human environment that the congregation will pass on their way to other spaces. This expansion not only creates new space but also changes the energy and usefulness of the existing space, connecting the two.

Palo Verde Library &
Maryvale Community Center
Phoenix, Arizona

EXERCISING THE MIND AND BODY In the late 1950s, developer John F. Long and architect Victor Gruen developed the master planned community of Maryvale, Arizona. Maryvale was the first post-war housing community, along with Levittown, New York, to revolutionize the home building industry.

The city of Phoenix proposed to reinvigorate the heart of Maryvale with a new 16,000-square-foot library and a 27,000-square-foot community center. The innovative mixed-use building program incorporates the existing pool while maintaining as much of Maryvale Park as feasible. The client wanted the park, library, and community center to be visible from the street, announcing their civic mission.

The new Palo Verde Library & Maryvale Community Center, designed by Gould Evans in association with Wendell Burnette, is a multi-use facility highlighted by a large public collections area, a 150-seat auditorium, and a collegiate-scale gymnasium. Through proximity to the street and transparency of program, the library volume reads as the exercise of the mind while the community center, park, and pool read as the exercise of the body. This mind/body dialogue resonates between two equally scaled column-free building volumes that incorporate the library collection and gymnasium. Each volume is a clear-span space, top- and bottom-lit for balanced daylight. The ball-field side of the complex is a series of masonry forms predicated on the existing masonry pool house. Dedicated parking lots are accessed along street frontage with dappled shade provided by a grove of Palo Verde trees.

Through form, daylighting, mechanical strategies, and material choices, all guided by the LEED Rating System, the design intent is environmentally responsible. For instance, cork floor tiles, a rapidly renewable resource, and a reference to the old Carnegie Libraries, are used throughout the 10,000-square-foot open collections area on a shallow, raised floor, which allows complete data and power flexibility. The gym/dance floors are made from rubber trees that were no longer productive. The library interior walls are sanded OSB (recycled aspen wood flakes) that resemble handmade paper books. The building simultaneously reads as bold and quiet, recording the range of light that epitomizes its place in the desert. Careful planning and material selection ensures that this remains the "green heart" of Maryvale, as well as being an understated but powerful presence in the community.

Riverside School for the Arts
Riverside, California

PORTAL TO ART   The Riverside Community College, the University of California at Riverside, and the Riverside Unified School District have joined forces to create a new school for the arts—a learning environment that fosters arts education and integrates design, performance, and visual arts with liberal arts and sciences. The mission is to nurture students, through the process of developing advanced levels of critical thinking, artistic achievement, and technical ability, as artists and creative members of our global culture.

This will be a place for students to learn to choreograph and compose, not just learn how to dance or play violin. Rather than operating within the conventional categories of music, dance, theater, art, and writing, the curricular areas are conceptualized with more inclusive terms such as sound, movement, and narrative in the performance domain. This conceptual tilt acknowledges that artists are increasingly defined more by their concepts than their tools, and ensures that RSA does not duplicate the current programs at the partner institutions.

The site is in the historic Raincross district of downtown Riverside. Through extensive community workshops and design discussions, the architects defined a design approach and spatial and aesthetic moves that would integrate with the neighborhood's historic Spanish mission style without imitating it.

The building is envisioned as a permeable portal to art, a kind of arts-infused, 24-hour crossroads for students and the community. It will exude an understanding of how it will be used, at what times of the day or week, and by whom. Daytime is a teaching and learning time—the classroom mode. Afternoon and dusk are transition periods, when the space mutates to allow for collaboration and ad hoc interactions; studio spaces evolve into display spaces merging video, sound, movement narrative, and writing. By evening, the time for performance has arrived—the formal community interface.

The building addresses the dense neighborhood on one side and White Park on the other side; these two entrances are linked through the building. The ground floor includes large public areas, including performance spaces, lobby, and galleries. The second floor includes classroom space, offices, and student services. The top floor is a studio that can be subdivided and includes an exterior courtyard "white box" theater as counterpoint to the black box performance space below.

Bentonville High School
Bentonville, Arkansas

INSPIRING SPACES This community's school district is experiencing rapid growth; enrollment projections indicated a need for a new 266,000-square-foot high school. This need impacted the current high school's distribution of grade levels. Ultimately, the new high school will house grades 11 through 12 of the 3,600-student community; it will be a center for art, science, and technology for the northwest region of Arkansas.

The project is a collaboration between Hight Jackson and Gould Evans. The design goal was to create a school centered on inspiring spaces. Two methods were employed to achieve this goal. The first is a macro-level organization of the building around a courtyard to alleviate a massiveness of scale due to the program, provide windows into every classroom, and create a clear visual entry point to unify the campus.

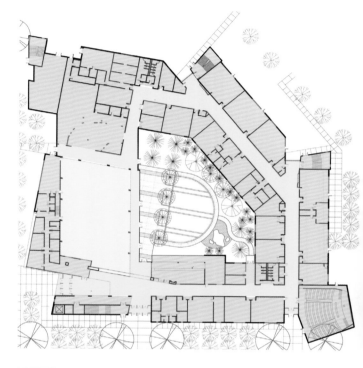

The second method for achieving inspiring spaces focuses on the classroom corridors. Early in the project, it was decided to arrange program spaces with breaks in classroom wings. The intent was twofold: to allow day-lighting into the heart of the building and to provide public non-circulation spaces off of the main corridors. Several functions were considered for these areas (blending zones, seating areas, cyber connections). They were understood by the design team as spaces for unconventional thought within the routine of daily school life. The breaks thus become display nodes that celebrate the work of the school in each zone (science, art, humanities). Using a consistent palette of ceramic tiled walls, glass displays, and sloped ceilings, these spaces are woven together throughout the building.

Key features include a three-story academic wing with day-lighting to all classroom spaces, a central courtyard with direct access from the commons, a multi-story media center, science labs, and a 200-seat lecture hall on the main level. At the main entry, a central stair tower was created to provide a clearly visible entry point for the school. The entry lobby serves as a large break separating the stair tower from the commons area. A three-story tile display wall acts as a separator at the ground floor level between the public areas and the school commons. The major public spaces (media center, commons, lobby) are hinged off of the wall as well. On the campus level, the wall serves as the first public display zone, which is also a visual clue for the breaks throughout the building.

The Power of We

Throughout this book and in our practice on a daily basis, principals and other leaders of Gould Evans use the word "we," because the activity of our firm is inherently collective and collaborative. The word often refers to a broad group of people that includes our clients, the building's community of users and neighbors, consultants, and other people outside the firm who bring important perspectives and insights to bear on our process and the work.

"We" always refers to numerous people within the firm. We have been inspired by the energy and talent of our associates; together we have refined our vision and values and a set of beliefs that drive our work every day.

Together, we believe in design rigor and relevance; cooperation and collaboration between people, teams, and offices; focus on the client; social embeddedness; and the power and possibility of the individual.

Since the firm's founding in 1974, we have worked with nearly 800 people in the firm, and thousands more beyond it. The strength of our work and the success of the firm are due in large part to this incredible collection of people, minds, and ideas. We are grateful for their contributions, which have resulted in powerful work, strong client relationships, and a foundation for a very exciting future.

Farhana Ali
Chris Andersen
Chris Armer
Linda Arvesen
Jocelyn Ashby
Brian Avery
Robert Aydlett
Irina Barboutis
Donna Barry
Ekaterina Barybina
Jenell Bass
Rob Beishline
Leo Berkey
Rachel Bias
Teri Bishop Price
Holly Black Irvine
Scott Blackford
Julie Bower
Margaret Bowker
Jason Boyer
Scott Branton
Tom Brenneis
Chris Brewster
Kip Brown
Laura Brunow
Greg Buchanan
Claudia Bullmore
Andrew Burge
Cyndia Cameron
Steve Carpenter
Angela Carroll
Seth Cavin
Cindy Childers
Thomas Chinnock
Jackson Clark
Steve Clark
Robert Clement
Sammey Collins
Shawn Croissant
John Curran Jr.
Dave Davis
Nancy Davis
Kim Del Rance

Tara Delgado
John Dimmel
Denise DiPiazzo
Becky DiRe Mullins
Doug Doering
Ray Dory
Butch Dougherty
Kelly Dreyer
Steve Duncan
Chris Dyroff
Liz Edmonds
Karen Eichenberger
Manuel Estrada, Jr.
David Evans
Melissa Farling
Jessica Flores
Brian Flowers
Lucy Flynn
Jason Foote
Deb Ford
Caroline Foster
Charles Gaddis
Brandon Gainey
Jennifer Galt
Ron Geren
Melisa Gillen
Bob Gould
Karen Gould
Kira Gould
Chad Greer
Donna Griffin
David Grimes
Mike Gruhala
Brian Hamilton
Basil Harb
Jim Harrington
Steve Harrington
Becky Hawkins
Shane Hawkins
Steve Heilman
Raina Heinrich
Everett Henderson, Jr.
Barbara Hendricks

Stacy Heuer
Jayne Higdon
Stephen Hopkins
Kyle Houston
Rick Howell
Jane Huesemann
Greg Hugeback
Trudi Hummel
Connie Jiang
Reid Johnson
Carrie Jones
Brandon Kent
Jason Kersley
Stacee Kersley
Teresa Kingsley
Tim Kitchens
Scott Klaus
Walter Knight
Rich Kniss
Dave Knopick
Kathy Krzeminski
Chet LaBruyere
Brad Lang
Glen LeRoy
Jeff Lewis
Tim Lies
Judith Loehmann
Mike Loesch
Mindy Looney
Eric Looney
Betsy Lynch
Carrie Mabee
Patrick Magness
Blaine Martin
Carol Martin Tracy
Rachael Mathey
Chris Mayor
Mike McAtee
John McClain
Peggy McDonough
Greg McDowell, Jr.
Kurt McGrew
Jaime McGrew

Brenda Moon
Eric Morehouse
Kelly Morgan
Fritz Morton
Lana Mosesova
Kaylyn Munro
Joel Natzke
Scott Neet
Barbara Newby
Patti Ann Nichols
Laura Nies
Adam Odgers
Katrina O'Rourke
David Parks
Brett Payton
Ana Paz
John Peter
Jose Pombo
Bob Radford, III
Kristy Reeves
David Reid
Tom Reilly
Libby Rivers
Theresa Roach
Sarah Roads
Jessie Robertson
Anthony Rohr
Adriana Rojas
Justin Roth
Kenichi Sato
Jim Schraeder
Deb Seeman
Robert Setterburg
Krista Shepherd
Tamara Shroll
Jay Silverberg
Jeet Singh
Henry Sipos
Bri Smathers
Graham Smith
Mark Smith
Brie Smith
Joe Smith

Ryan Smith
Chris Sogas
Tom Solon
Scott Stalcup
Adam Sterns
Gary Stoddard
Jean Stoverink
Dennis Strait
Adam Strong
Alice Sung
Mickey Sutliff
Katelyn Swezy
Marcus Thomas
Brian Tong
Jesus Torres-Sosa
Martin Tovrea
Jonathan Tramba
Katie Trenkle
Alain Valdes
Debby Vaughan
Matt Veasman
Ouvieng Voravong
Steve Vukelich
Corey Walker
John Ware
Sara Wavada
Roger Webb, II
Jim Wehmueller
Michael Welch
Robert Whitman
John Wilkins
Dave Willard
Tanya Wilson
Miya Wilson
Jonathan Wirth
Tara Wood
Tim Woofter
Rebecca Young
Kris Young
Sean Zaudke
Dan Zeller
Greg Zielinski

Acknowledgements & Credits

COMPLETED WORK

Harry S. Truman Presidential Library & Museum
Independence, Missouri

client: General Services Administration
completion date: October 2001

general contractor: Walton Construction
federal oversight: National Archives and Records
    Administration
exhibit designer: Chermayeff & Geismar
structural engineer: Shafer, Kline & Warren
mechanical engineer: Shafer, Kline & Warren
landscape architect: Gould Evans
signage design: Gould Evans

photographer: Mike Sinclair

Stevie Eller Dance Theatre
Tucson, Arizona

client: University of Arizona
completion date: July 2003

general contractor: CF Jordan Construction
structural engineer: Rudow & Berry
mechanical engineer: Bridgers & Paxton
landscape architect: Ten Eyck Landscape Architects
signage design: Gould Evans
rigging and lighting: Landry & Bogan

photographer: Timothy Hursley

Cerner Corporation Campus
Kansas City, Missouri

client: Cerner Corporation
completion date: October 2002

general contractor: J.E. Dunn Construction
structural engineer: Page McNaghten Associates
mechanical engineer: Lankford & Associates
civil engineer: Shafer, Kline & Warren
landscape architect: Gould Evans
signage design: Gould Evans
metal work: A2MG, Inc. (Baker-Smith Sheet Metal)
acoustics: Acoustical Design Group
glass: Architectural Glass Engineering
fountain design: HydroDramatics

photographers: Michael Spillers, Neil Sommers

Adelphi Commons Sorority Housing
Tempe, Arizona

client: Arizona State University / Century Development
completion date: 2001

general contractor: Swinerton & Walberg Company
mechanical engineer: Bridgers & Paxton
structural engineer: Rudow & Berry
civil engineer: Evans Kuhn Associates
landscape architect: Ten Eyck Landscape Architects
signage design: Gould Evans

photographer: Bill Timmerman

First Covenant Church
Salina, Kansas

client: First Covenant Church
completion date: May 2004

general contractor: Busboom & Rauh Construction Co.
structural engineer: Bob D. Campbell & Company
mechanical engineer: Bucher, Willis & Ratliff
civil engineer/landscape architect: Earles & Riggs Inc.
acoustics: Acoustical Design Group, Inc.

photographer: Michael Spillers

College of Business Administration
Tampa, Florida

client: University of South Florida
completion date: January 2005

general contractor: PPI
structural engineer: Master Consulting Engineers, Inc.
mechanical engineer: Tilden Lobnitz Cooper
civil engineer: EMK Consultants of Florida
landscape architect: Hardeman-Kempton & Associates
signage design: Gould Evans

photographer: George Cott

Eccles Center for Performing Arts
& Horne School of Music
Ephraim, Utah

client: State of Utah
completion date: November 2003

general contractor: Layton Construction
structural engineer: Reaveley Engineers & Associates
mechanical engineer: Spectrum Engineers
civil engineer: Van Boerum & Frank Associates
electrical engineer/A/V: BNA Consulting Engineers
acoustics: Dohn Associates
rigging and lighting: Landry + Bogan

photographer: Timothy Hursley

Grandview Community Center
Grandview, Missouri

client: City of Grandview
completion date: 2004

associate architect: Ankeny Kell Architects

construction manager: McCown Gordon Construction
structural engineer: Bob D. Campbell & Company
mechanical/electrical/civil engineer: Henderson Engineers
landscape architect: Gould Evans
pool consultant: Water's Edge Aquatic Design
signage design: Gould Evans

The Biodesign Institute
Tempe, Arizona

client: The Biodesign Institute at Arizona State University
completion date: December 2004

associate architect: Lord Aeck & Sargent

general contractor: Sundt Construction/DPR Construction
structural engineer: Paragon Structural Design
mechanical engineer/security consultant: Newcomb & Boyd
civil engineer: Evans Kuhn Associates
landscape architect: Ten Eyck Landscape Architects
signage design: Gould Evans
vibration control/acoustics: Colin Gordon & Associates
EMI: VitaTech

photographer: Timothy Hursley

Baron BMW
Merriam, Kansas

client: Baron Automotive Group
completion date: August 2000

general contractor: Walton Construction
structural engineer: Ali Harris Company
mechanical engineer: Henderson Engineers
civil engineer: SK Design Group
landscape architect: Gould Evans
signage design: Gould Evans
lighting design: Yarnell Associates

photographers: Mike Sinclair, Walter Knight

Rinker Hall School of Building Construction
Gainesville, Florida

client: University of Florida
completion date: January 2003

associate architect: Croxton Collaborative

general contractor: Centex Rooney Construction Company
structural engineer: Walter P. Moore
mechanical engineer: Lehr Associates
civil engineer: Brown & Cullen, Inc.
landscape architect: McClain Design Group, Inc.
signage design: Gould Evans

photographers: Timothy Hursley, George Cott

Johnson County Library, Blue Valley
Overland Park, Kansas

client: Johnson County Library System
completed: July 2000

general contractor: McPherson Contractors, Inc.
structural engineer: Bob D. Campbell & Company
mechanical engineer: Henthorn, Sandmeyer & Company
civil engineer: Shafer, Kline & Warren
landscape architect: Gould Evans
signage design: Gould Evans
acoustics: Acoustical Design Group

photographer: Mike Sinclair

Pearson Hall School of Education
Lawrence, Kansas

client: University of Kansas
completion date: August 2001

general contractor: Ferrell Construction Company
structural engineer: Bob D. Campbell & Company
mechanical engineer: Latimer, Sommers & Associates
civil engineer: LandPlan Engineering
landscape architect: Gould Evans
acoustics: Acoustical Design Group

photographer: Michael Spillers

First United Methodist Church
Blue Springs, Missouri

client: First United Methodist Church
completion date: August 2001

general contractor: Meyer Brothers Building Company
structural engineer: Structural Engineering Associates
mechanical engineer: W.L. Cassell & Associates
civil engineer: SK Design Group
acoustics: Acoustical Design Group

photographer: Mike Sinclair

Athletes' Performance Institute
Tempe, Arizona

client: Athletes' Performance, Inc.
completion date: June 2001

general contractor: Heller Construction
structural engineer: Rudow & Berry
mechanical engineer: Kunka Engineering
civil engineer: CMX Engineering
electrical engineer: Associated Engineering
landscape architect: Ten Eyck Landscape Architects
signage design: Adidas America, Inc. / Gould Evans

photographer: Bill Timmerman

Cedar City Library
Cedar City, Utah

client: City of Cedar City
completion date: August, 2003

general contractor: Blackburn and Associates
structural engineer: Reaveley Engineers
mechanical engineer: Spectrum Engineers
civil engineer: Leslie & Associates
landscape architect: SGE & Associates
signage design: Gould Evans

photographer: Rob Beishline

East Campus Student Union
Mesa, Arizona

client: Arizona State University (East Campus)
completion date: September 2004

general contractor: Turner Construction
structural engineer: Rudow & Berry
mechanical engineer: Kunka Engineering
electrical engineer: Associated Engineering
landscape architect: Ten Eyck Landscape Architects
signage design: Gould Evans
foodservice: Hamilton Associates
bookstore design: Kremer Associates

photographer: Matt Winquist

Love of Christ Church Center for Compassion
Mesa, Arizona

client: Love of Christ Lutheran Church
completion date: January 2003

general contractor: Concord General Contracting
structural engineer: Rudow & Berry
mechanical engineer: Bridgers & Paxton
civil engineering: Evans Kuhn Associates
electrical engineer: Associated Engineering
landscape architect: Ten Eyck Landscape Archtitects
A/V and acoustics: Riske & Associates

photographer: Bill Timmerman

SALT Center
Tucson, Arizona

client: University of Arizona
completion date: 2001

general contractor: Lang Wyatt Construction
structural engineer: Rudow & Berry
mechanical engineer: Bridgers & Paxton
civil engineer / landscape architect: Stantec Consulting
electrical engineer / voice & data systems: Associated
    Engineering
signage design: Gould Evans

photographer: Bill Timmerman

BleuJacket Restaurant
Lawrence, Kansas

client: Fleur-de-lis Restaurant Group
completed: December 2000

general contractor: Harris Construction
mechanical engineer: BC Engineers
food service consultant: Santee/Becker Associates

photographer: Mike Sinclair

ON THE BOARDS

St. Paul's United Methodist Church
Lenexa, Kansas

client: St. Paul's United Methodist Church
completion date: 2005

general contractor: Harmon Construction Inc.
structural engineer: Haris Engineering
mechanical/electrical/plumbing engineer: Latimer,
    Sommers & Associates
environmental / civil engineer: Tetra Tech EM Inc.
landscape architect: Patti Banks Associates

Arts & Technology Complex
Overland Park, Kansas

client: Johnson County Community College
projected completion date: 2007

associate architect (museum): Kyu Sung Woo
    Architects

construction manager: J.E. Dunn Construction
structural engineer: Walter P. Moore & Associates
mechanical engineer: Smith & Boucher, Inc.
civil engineer: Kaw Valley Engineering
landscape architect: Gould Evans
technology consultant: KJWW Engineering Consultants
food service: Santee/Becker
lighting consultant: Derek Porter Studio
acoustics: Acoustical Design Group

renderings: Arnold Imaging

Indian Creek Community Church
Olathe, Kansas

client: Indian Creek Community Church of God, Inc.
projected completion date: 2006

general contractor: MPW Construction
structural engineer: Structural Engineering Associates, Inc.
mechanical engineer: Larson Binkley, Inc.
civil engineer: SK Design Group, Inc.
landscape architect: Gould Evans
lighting design: Derek Porter Studio
acoustics: Acoustical Design Group, Inc.
fountain consultant: Hydro Dramatics
tile and fountain artist: Fired Earth Designs LTD

Palo Verde Library & Maryvale Community Center
Phoenix, Arizona

client: City of Phoenix
projected completion date: 2006

associate architect: Wendell Burnette Architects

general contractor: Smith Construction Management
structural engineer: Rudow + Berry
mechanical engineer: Kunka Engineering
civil engineer: WRG Design
electrical engineer: Associated Engineering
landscape architect: Ten Eyck Landscape Architects
signage design: Thinking Caps
lighting design: Horton Lees Brogden Lighting Design
acoustics: Wardin Cockriel Associates
historian: Nancy Dallett, Projects in the Public Interest

Riverside School for the Arts
Riverside, California

client: Riverside Community College District
projected completion date: 2008

associate architect: tBP Architects

structural engineer: John A. Martin & Associates, Inc.
mechanical engineer: B&P Engineering
civil engineer: KCT Consultants
electrical engineer: FBA Engineering
signage design: Gould Evans Associates

Bentonville High School
Bentonville, Arkansas

client: Bentonville Unified School District 6
projected completion date: 2006

associate architect (project architect): Hight-Jackson
    Associates

First published in the United States of America by Edizioni
Press, Inc. 469 West 21st Street New York, New York 10011
www.edizionipress.com

ISBN: 1-931536-46-5

Library of Congress Catalogue Card Number: 2006921222

Printed in China

Design: Gary Kon

Editor: Nancy Sul

Front Cover: Stevie Eller Dance Theatre,
Photographed by Timothy Hursley